THE BAREFOOT BOOK OF

Stories from the Stars

Myths of the Zodiac

For Catherine Davis, with love and thanks - J.M.
For Emily and Jessica - J.S.B.

Barefoot Books Ltd
PO Box 95
Kingswood
Bristol BS15 5BH

This book has been printed on 100% acid-free paper

First published in Great Britain in 1996 by Barefoot Books Ltd

Printed in Hong Kong by South Sea International Press

ISBN 1 898000 59 X

To darling Maxim
Wishing you a very
Happy Christmas
1996.
With all our love
Grandma and
Dadan

THE BAREFOOT BOOK OF

Stories from the Stars

Myths of the Zodiac

COMPILED BY

Juliet Sharman Burke

ILLUSTRATED BY

Jackie Morris

BAREFOOT BOOKS

BATH

Contents

About the Stars of the Zodiac
5

The Planets
6

Jason and the Golden Fleece (Aries – 21 March-20 April)
8

Theseus and the Minotaur (Taurus – 21 April-21 May)
16

Castor and Pollux (Gemini – 22 May-21 June)
24

Herakles and the Hydra (Cancer – 22 June-23 July)
30

Herakles and the Nemean Lion (Leo – 24 July-23 August)
36

Demeter and Persephone (Virgo – 24 August-23 September)
40

The Golden Scales of Dike (Libra – 24 September-23 October)
48

Orion and the Scorpion (Scorpio – 24 October-22 November)
52

Chiron the Centaur (Sagittarius – 23 November-21 December)
56

The Birth of Zeus (Capricorn – 22 December-20 January)
62

Ganymede the Cup Bearer (Aquarius – 21 January-19 February)
68

Aphrodite and the Fish (Pisces – 20 February-20 March)
72

Notes on the Sunsigns
78

About the Stars of the Zodiac

Have you ever stood outside on a clear night and looked up at the stars? It is a wonderful experience. At first, those twinkling pinpoints of light in the night sky can all look the same, but if you keep looking, you will see that some of them make patterns.

Many years ago, our ancestors divided the stars into groups and drew imaginary pictures around them. They noticed that the movement of the sun, moon and stars across the sky affected life on earth. The sun and the moon marked out the time spans that became months, and twelve particular patterns of stars, or constellations, appeared regularly each year. These twelve constellations make up the zodiac.

Viewed from earth, the sun appeared to spend about a month passing through each constellation, so the twelve zodiacal constellations reflecting the changing seasons of the year came to be known as sunsigns. The planets, too, appeared to move at varying rates through the backdrop of the constellations.

In ancient Greece, where the word 'zodiac' comes from, each constellation was described and remembered through a myth. In this book you will read these myths and learn about the qualities that are associated with each sunsign.

The Planets

The gods and goddesses of ancient Greece were associated with the planets, which we know today by their Roman names. Eight planets are listed here, though not all of them were known to the ancient Greeks – Uranus was discovered in 1781 and Pluto in 1930.

MERCURY, the fastest-moving planet, was named after the Greek god Hermes (Her-mees), messenger of the gods. He wore winged sandals and a broad-brimmed hat, which was also winged so as to help speed him on his errands. Hermes was well known for his quick wit and his clever ways of getting out of mischief.

VENUS, the bright, brilliant-white planet, was named after Aphrodite (Af-row-die-tee), the Greek goddess of love. She was born of sea foam and was as delicately beautiful as foam itself. Her chariot, drawn by doves or swans, was decorated with fruit and flowers. Aphrodite possessed a magic girdle which had the power to make all men fall in love with her.

MARS, the red planet, was named after the Greek god Ares (Air-ees). He was the quarrelsome god of war, feared for his violence and cruelty. He was seven hundred feet tall, with a shock of red hair, and was always looking for trouble. Only when he was with the lovely Aphrodite did his temper improve!

JUPITER is the largest planet of the solar system, named after the Greek god Zeus (Zeeoose) – the great father of all. Zeus was all-powerful, obeyed by gods and mortals alike. He had a good sense of humour, but everyone feared him when he grew angry. He always carried a handful of thunderbolts to throw around in case anyone vexed him. Thunder and lightning on earth was a sure sign that Zeus was not happy!

SATURN, the second-largest planet, was named after Zeus's father, the Earth god Cronus. Cronus is sometimes shown carrying a sickle, which he used in his battle to overthrow his tyrannical father, Ouranus (yoo-ra-nus).

URANUS, the greeny-blue planet, was named after Cronus's father. This name meant 'sky' and he was married to Gaia (Guy-a), or Mother Earth.

NEPTUNE, the bright-blue planet, was named after Poseidon (Po-side-on), the Greek god of the sea. Poseidon lived in a shell palace beneath the waves, adorned with corals and sea flowers. Carrying his three-pronged trident, he rode in a chariot drawn by dolphins and sea-horses. Poseidon had a hot temper and when he flew into a rage he would stir up the waves with his magic trident.

PLUTO is the planet named after the Greek god Hades (Hay-dees), the gloomy lord of the dead, whose kingdom was known as the Underworld. His throne was made of ebony and his chariot was drawn by coal-black horses. He had a special helmet that made him invisible when he wore it, so that he could move among people without them seeing him. Hades was very wealthy indeed yet his kingdom was dark and cheerless.

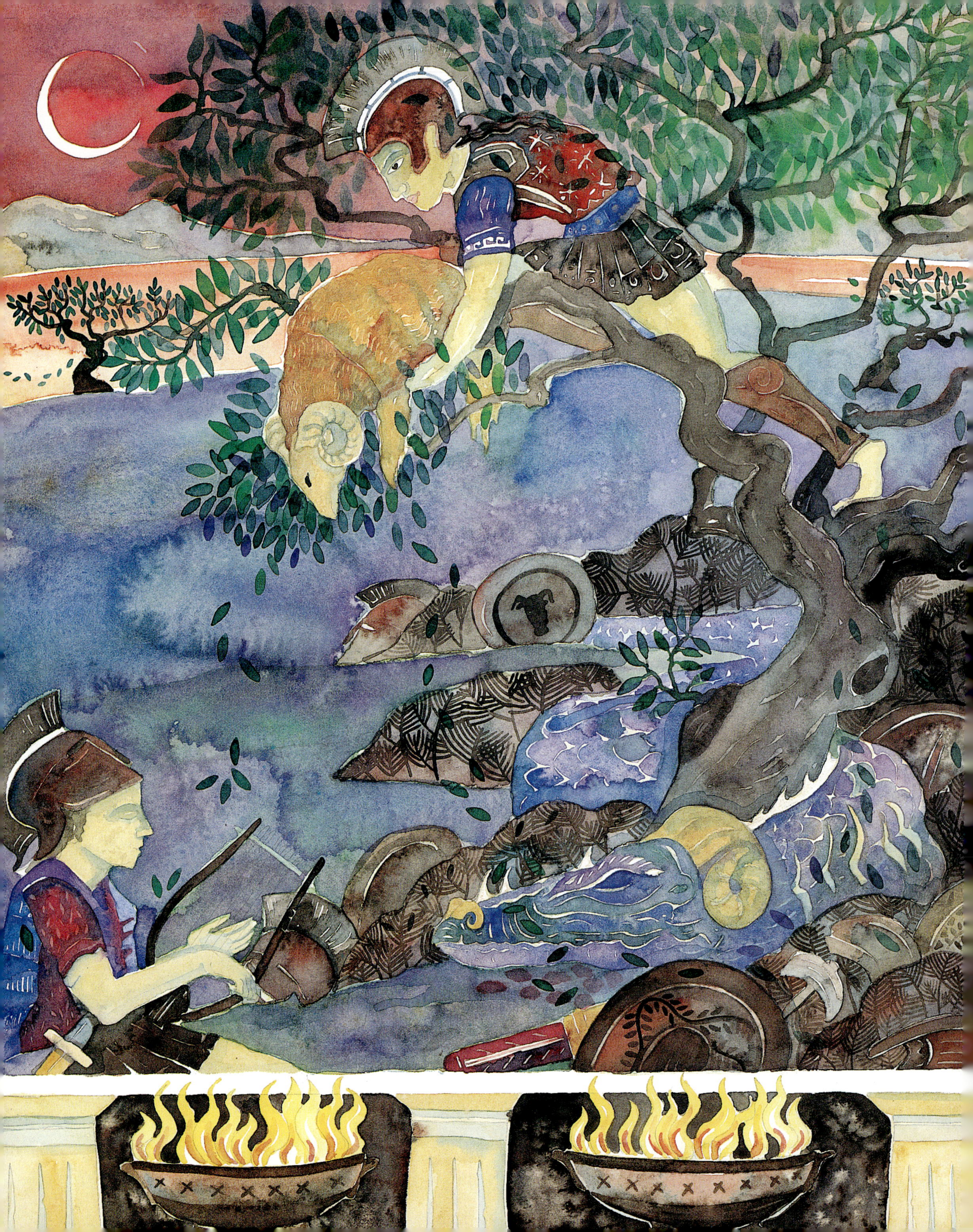

Jason and the Golden Fleece

ARIES (21 MARCH–20 APRIL)

This is the story of the first sign of the zodiac – that is, the sign that marks the beginning of spring and the start of a new cycle of life. It tells of how a ram found its way into the stars.

Jason was the rightful heir to the throne of Iolcus (Ee-ol-kus) but his wicked Uncle Pelias (Peel-ee-ass) had stolen the crown, killing Jason's father. Pelias believed that Jason was dead, too – but he was alive. The centaur Chiron (Ky-ron) had taken care of the boy from babyhood in a secret cave.

Being wise and good, Chiron taught Jason the value of courage and strength. On Jason's sixteenth birthday Chiron called him, saying, 'Jason, you are old enough to know that you are the true king of Iolcus. Your Uncle Pelias murdered your father and he thinks you are dead too. The time has come for you to claim the throne and avenge your father's death.'

Jason, horrified and excited by what Chiron told him, set off without delay to take revenge on his uncle. On the way to Iolcus, he came to a fast-running river where an old lady sat sadly by the bank.

'Please, kind sir,' she begged, 'won't you carry me across? You are young and strong, while I am old and feeble.'

Jason gladly offered to help, but the old lady was heavier than he thought; he staggered and almost fell, losing a sandal in the muddy river bed while wading through the icy waters. None the less, he managed the crossing. As soon he reached the other side, the old lady turned into the goddess Hera (Hear-a), radiant queen of heaven.

'Jason,' said she, 'you are brave but also kind. You were willing to help me and now I am going to help you become one of the most famous heroes in all Greece!'

Jason wondered how this might come about, but didn't give it much thought as he continued eagerly on his journey.

Meanwhile King Pelias sat uncomfortably on the throne in Iolcus. His life as king had not been very contented. An oracle had warned him to beware of a man wearing only one sandal – a man who would bring about his death. After he heard that, he had never stopped worrying and always looked at the feet of every stranger he met.

Not long after his meeting with Hera, Jason strode into Iolcus, heading straight for the palace.

When Pelias was greeted by this stranger wearing only one sandal, he was very alarmed. But he decided not to quarrel with him, particularly when he learned that the youth was actually his nephew.

But Pelias was crafty, and after promising that he would be happy to give the crown to Jason, he added, 'Now the kingdom is to be yours, Jason, don't you think it would be much improved if you had something really special to honour it – like the Golden Fleece of Colchis?' And he told Jason about the fleece that hung on an enchanted tree at the world's end, guarded by a fierce dragon which never slept.

Of course, he said nothing about how many people before Jason had tried to capture the fleece, nor how all had failed, meeting their death in the attempt.

Jason wasted no time. He instructed a master shipbuilder, recommended by Hera, to build him a huge ship with fifty oars, which he called the Argo. Next, he gathered together a band of brave young men, each with a distinctive talent. Among them were Herakles, the strongest man on Earth; the twins Castor and Pollux, who were fearless fighters; and Orpheus (Oar-fee-us), the famous musician who played the lyre so sweetly that even the rocks and trees would get up and follow him. Jason and his crew, whom he named the Argonauts, set sail for Colchis with high hopes.

Hera had provided the ship with a magic figurehead, shaped like a woman, to adorn its prow. This special figurehead had the power of speech, which immediately proved very useful. Jason had been in such high spirits about gathering the crew together and building a splendid boat that he set sail in great haste, forgetting, amid all the excitement, where they were going. He crept forward and whispered to the wooden lady at the ship's prow, 'Can you guide me? I don't know the way!'

To his huge relief, this advice came from the wooden figure: 'Sail to the south and seek out the blind King Phineas (Fin-ee-us). He will guide you.'

So they went south until they reached Phineas's kingdom. The king told them which way to go and warned them of the sea-peril ahead. His advice proved sound, and once they were safely through the terrible Crashing Rocks, they soon reached the shores of Colchis.

King Aeetes (A-ee-tees), ruler of the land, watched the crew arrive. He was accustomed to strangers seeking the legendary Golden Fleece, but these men looked stronger and more determined than usual.

Like Jason's Uncle Pelias, Aeetes decided to set Jason a task which he believed to be impossible, hoping that this would easily get rid of him.

'Well, Jason,' said the king, 'I reckon you can have the precious Golden Fleece if you are first able to harness my two fiercest bulls. They breathe fire, of course, but that shouldn't worry a hero like you. Then I want you to use the bulls to plough a field and sow a crop of dragon's teeth. These will instantly grow into armed soldiers, but a gallant fellow like yourself should be able to fight them off, eh?' And Aeetes laughed heartily, and left

Jason alone to decide how to set about this daunting task.

While Jason was wondering what to do, Medea (Med-ee-ah), Aeetes's daughter, entered the room. Medea had waist-length, raven-black hair and great black eyes which flashed like fire. She wore a gorgeous crimson silk robe that shimmered as she walked, and carried a fan made out of peacock feathers. Hera called on Aphrodite for help, and the goddess of love instructed her son Eros to fire a gold-tipped arrow at Medea's heart. Instantly the king's daughter fell in love with Jason.

Smiling warmly, Medea approached Jason, who did not know, of course, that she was also a witch and an enchantress.

'Here, Jason,' she said in velvety tones, handing him a little box and a shining silver helmet. 'I want to help you. My father has set you a very difficult task, but it is not impossible. This ointment will protect you from heat and flame for one day. Before you harness the fire-breathing bulls, just spread it all over your body. Don't worry about the dragon's teeth either: just sow them, and when the soldiers appear, all you have to do is toss this helmet into their midst – they will fight each other and you can slip away!'

Jason did just as Medea advised. The ointment gave complete protection against the fiery bulls; the helmet distracted the attention of the soldiers; and so he completed his tasks – much to the fury and amazement of King Aeetes.

'I shall give you the Golden Fleece tomorrow,' Aeetes muttered angrily. But he did not plan to keep his promise. Instead, he plotted to

murder the Argonauts and burn their ship. Once again, Medea came to Jason's rescue. She crept into his room in the middle of the night.

'Quick, Jason, there is no time to lose,' she whispered. 'If we are to get the Fleece, it must be tonight, for my father plans to kill you all in the morning. But promise me one thing first: that you will marry me and take me back with you.'

Although Jason liked Medea and was grateful to her for her help, he realised that her magic was powerful and was a bit nervous at the idea of marrying a witch; but at that moment he would probably have promised anybody anything, and so he agreed to marry her on their return to Iolcus.

'Call Orpheus, the musician,' said Medea, 'and follow me.'

Medea led Jason and Orpheus through the sinister moonlit garden at the world's end, until they came to the place where the Golden Fleece glimmered in the darkness. But around the tree from which it hung was coiled the great serpent's tail of the dragon that never slept – larger and more terrible than any other dragon in the world.

'Play and sing,' hissed Medea to Orpheus, who gently plucked the strings on his lyre and sang a sweet, low lullaby. The whole garden slowly relaxed: the blades of grass and flowers bent downwards, the night-time animals closed their eyes. Even Jason started yawning. He only managed to stay awake because Medea had sprinkled him with magic dust. Even the dragon relaxed, its fearsome head drooping on to a bed of sleeping silken-red poppies.

Then Jason nimbly climbed the tree and quickly unhooked the Fleece. Medea called upon Hecate (Hec-a-tee), the immortal queen of witches and sorceresses, to darken the moon, and the night closed over Colchis like a black cloak. Carrying the Fleece as their only means of light, Jason, Medea and Orpheus crept out of the magic garden. As they left, the dragon woke from its charmed sleep and roared with rage, but it was too late. Jason, Medea and the Argonauts had escaped and were on their way back to Iolcus.

The journey home was long and arduous, and many years passed before at last the Argonauts saw their home again. As they stepped ashore carrying the Golden Fleece, they were hardly recognised by their friends. Pelias was now a very old man, still ruling the kingdom; but despite his earlier promise, he would not give up the throne to Jason.

Once again, Medea stepped in. This time she offered Pelias a magic potion, assuring him that it would make him young again. Knowing Medea's powers, Pelias believed her. But instead of bringing him youth, the potion sent him into a sleep from which he never woke up, so fulfilling the oracle which warned him that a one-sandalled man would bring about his death.

Once Jason had fulfilled his destiny and become king of Iolcus, Zeus put the ram's Golden Fleece up in the skies, where it appears as the constellation of Aries.

Theseus and the Minotaur

TAURUS (21 APRIL–21 MAY)

The image of the bull's head up in the sky has its origins in the legend of Theseus and the Minotaur.

Many years ago Minos was King of Crete. Like all those who lived on that island, he had a great admiration for bulls. One day, the god of the ocean, Poseidon, asked Minos to make him a gift of the best white bull in his herd. Minos hated to part with the best, so he foolishly gave the god his second-best bull, hoping that Poseidon would not notice. But, of course, the gods cannot be deceived, and Poseidon was very angry that Minos had dared to try to trick him.

The god of the ocean cursed King Minos's family, and as part of his punishment he caused Minos's wife to give birth to a horrible monster. It had the body of a man and the head of a bull, with a terrible appetite which could only be satisfied by eating young human flesh. The monster was called the Minotaur (My-no-tor).

King Minos was terribly ashamed and alarmed when he realised what had happened. In order to try to hide this monster, he called for his master craftsman, Daedalus (Die-da-lus).

'Make me a maze,' Minos commanded. 'And make it so complicated that no one can ever find the way out. I never want to see that Minotaur again!' Daedalus was very clever indeed and constructed an underground maze with a cave at its heart where the Minotaur was hidden away. It was known as the Labyrinth.

Twice a year, King Minos ordered the people of his subject cities across the sea to send seven of their young men and seven young women into the Labyrinth as food for the greedy Minotaur. Naturally the people of these cities were very unhappy about losing their children in this awful way, but none dared quarrel with their ruler. One year, King Minos commanded Athens to send fourteen fine young people to satisfy the Minotaur's hunger. Prince Theseus of Athens, a handsome and brave young man, thought that young Athenians should not be forced to meet such a dreadful fate, and begged his father, King Aegeus (Ee-gee-us), to let him try to slay the Minotaur.

'Father,' he begged, 'let me go as one of the seven young men sent for by Minos and I will kill the Minotaur myself!'

His father wept and said, 'No, no, I cannot agree. Please don't go Theseus – you will be killed! You are my only son and I love you more than life itself.'

But Theseus pleaded and argued and cajoled until his father finally gave in.

'All right, my son – I will allow it,' he sighed, sorrowfully. 'But I make one condition. You must set sail with the black sails of mourning on your ship, and if you are successful in your quest and you do manage to kill the beast, then change the sails to white ones before returning home. This way, I can watch for you on the harbour walls and will be warned whether you are dead or alive.'

Theseus agreed. Before a week had passed, he and his thirteen young companions embarked from Athens on a black-sailed ship.

Theseus was always quick to take up a challenge, but having arrived on Crete, even he began to wonder how he was to going to find his way into the Labyrinth, kill the beast and find his way out again alive. Yet he was the kind of person who always looked on the bright side of life.

'Never mind that I don't have a plan,' he told himself. 'I will trust to my luck and I am sure something will turn up.'

Before being fed to the Minotaur, the victims were always given a fine party at the palace, where games and lavish entertainment were laid on. They were allowed to take part in races and boxing, which they performed before the King and his court. In the audience was King Minos's daughter, Ariadne (A-ri-ad-nee), who sat watching Theseus's win each event. Ariadne was a very beautiful girl. Her thick dark hair fell down her back in flower-entwined curls and she wore a gown of soft damask rose.

As she watched Theseus compete so gallantly and win so effortlessly, Ariadne's heart opened up to him. Unable to bear the thought of him dying in that horrible Labyrinth, slain by that dreadful monster, she approached him after the games were over.

'Prince Theseus,' she whispered, 'I have a plan to help you.' And she drew him over to one side. 'Take this ball of golden thread,' she continued softly, 'and slowly unravel it as you walk through the maze. No one has ever found their way out of the Labyrinth alive, but the golden twine will help you to find your way back to me.'

Emboldened by her love, Theseus followed Ariadne's advice. The next day, he entered the dark, dank Labyrinth alone, securely tying one end of the golden thread to the inside of the heavy door, which was shut behind him. Carefully unwinding the ball of thread, he made his way through the gloomy passages, which twisted and turned, this way and that, leading him up and down in all directions.

At last he came to the great cave at the very heart of the Labyrinth. He heard the rumble of snoring and could dimly make out the shape of a great beast fast asleep. Although he crept towards the monster as quietly as any mouse, the Minotaur awoke at the slight sound, aroused too by the smell of a human being, and let out an alarming roar of hunger. He was a fearsome creature to behold, with the body of a mighty man, and the head and neck of a huge bull. His horns were long and razor-sharp; his skin, a dull yellow the colour of brass, was as tough as the toughest leather.

The fight that followed was ferocious and unyielding. At first the Minotaur fought unflinchingly, but Theseus was quick and clever, teasing the lumbering beast unmercifully. Being so agile, Theseus always escaped when the monster attacked, and gradually he managed to exhaust him. As the Minotaur began to droop, panting heavily, Theseus sprang at once onto his back, grabbing the thick parts of the beast's horns and forcing back his head until at last, with a mighty crack, his great neck broke and he lay dead.

Theseus picked up what remained of the ball of twine and, carefully rewinding it, made his way back. For, despite having killed the Minotaur, without his thin line of gold Theseus would have been well and truly lost.

Ariadne was waiting for him, overjoyed. 'Thank goodness you are alive!' she cried, hugging him tightly.

'Ariadne, I need to get home to my father,' said Theseus. 'I must let him know I am safe.'

'Then take me too,' she begged.

And so together they set sail for Athens.

What happened next is not quite clear. Some say that Theseus stopped loving Ariadne and deliberately left her behind on the island of Naxos, where they had stopped for a rest on their journey. Others say the god Dionysus (Dy-on-ee-sus) caught sight of Ariadne on the island and fell in love with her. He then cast a spell, making her fall into a charmed sleep so that she would forget all about Theseus and love him instead. Whatever the circumstances, Ariadne married Dionysus and they were very happy together. Many years later, when Ariadne died, Dionysus hurled the diamond-encrusted crown he had given her on their wedding day high up into the skies, where it turned into a circle of stars which is known today as the constellation of Corona Borealis.

As for Theseus, although he meant no harm, he was in such a hurry to get home that he quite forgot to change the sails from black to white. His father, King Aegeus, had spent many anxious days watching out for his son's safe return, and when he saw the ship approaching still with its black sails, he feared the worst and threw himself into the sea – now called the Aegean, after him.

A bull's head was placed in the stars by Zeus as a reminder of the origins of the island of Crete, and it became known as the constellation of Taurus.

Castor and Pollux

GEMINI (22 MAY–21 JUNE)

Castor and Pollux were twins, but not in an ordinary sense, for they had different fathers. They gave their name to the constellation of Gemini.

For some time the god Zeus had admired the lovely Queen Leda of Sparta, and he wanted to get to know her better. In order not to frighten her, he transformed himself into a dazzling white swan. In the course of time, Queen Leda produced two eggs.

One of the eggs contained a baby girl, who was named Helen (later to be known as the beautiful Helen of Troy), and a baby boy called Pollux. These two were the divine children of the god Zeus. Children born to the gods were immortal, which meant they would live for ever, while mortals would die eventually and be sent to the

Underworld. The other egg opened up to reveal another girl and boy – Clytemnestra (Kly-tem-nes-tra) and Castor – who were the mortal children of King Tyndareus (Tin-dar-ee-us), Leda's husband.

Despite the fact that one brother was divine and the other mortal, the twins Castor and Pollux were inseparable. They did everything together and loved each other dearly. As babies they played together and never quarrelled in the way that most brothers and sisters do. One never tried to be better than the other; they always wanted everything to be equal and fair. As they grew up they still longed to be together all the time, and if there was an adventure to be had, they went on it together; if there was a battle to fight, they fought it together. Because they were so close they were called by one name – the Dioscuri (Dye-os-cure-ee). The brothers both loved all kinds of sports. Pollux was particularly good at boxing and Castor was renowned for his skill and daring on horseback. They were always competing and winning prizes at the Olympic Games, but the one had no wish to do better than the other.

They shared everything – success or failure. They even looked exactly the same, and the only difference you might ever notice between them was that the face of Pollux bore scars from boxing. They dressed exactly the same: purple tunics, each with a half-eggshell and a star on his shield, each with a spear and an identical white horse.

They joined Jason's quest to find the Golden Fleece. He valued their company, not only because they were brave and valiant fighters, but also because they were able to calm the rough seas which threatened to capsize the Argo. Poseidon, the god of the ocean, had made Castor and Pollux joint saviours of shipwrecked sailors and granted them the power to send favourable winds whenever they wished, so they were most helpful on the Argonauts' voyage. Even to this day, the sight of the stars of the Dioscuri in the sky is regarded by sailors as an omen of good luck.

Unfortunately, one day the brothers quarrelled with another set of twins and became involved in a bitter fight. Castor, the mortal son of King Tyndareus, was killed, and was summoned to the Underworld.

Pollux was heartbroken, and prayed aloud to Zeus: 'Heavenly Father, do not let me live if I cannot be with my beloved brother!'

And Zeus replied, 'Very well, Pollux, if you do not wish to remain on Earth without Castor, come up to the heavens and live with us here.'

But Pollux still wept. 'No, heavenly Father,' he sobbed. 'I do not want to live for ever if it means being separated from my brother.'

Zeus was so touched by the twins' love and devotion for each other that he arranged for them to be together again. They could

divide their time between the heavens and the Underworld, spending one day high up in the divine home of the gods, Olympus, and the next deep beneath the Earth in the realm of Hades.

In further recognition of their brotherly love, he set their images among the stars as the constellation of Gemini so that they would never again be separated. They stand out as two equally bright stars in a constellation of weaker stars.

Herakles and the Hydra

CANCER (22 JUNE–23 JULY)

This story tells of how a crab found its way into the heavens.
It is told as part of the adventures of the great hero Herakles,
the strongest man on Earth.

Zeus wanted a son who was strong and fearless and one who could help him in his battles. An oracle told him that such a hero would be born into the royal family of Argolis. Zeus decided that he should be the father of this hero and that Alcmena (Alk-mee-na) of Argolis should be the mother. So he appeared to Alcmena in the shape of her own husband, and in due course the baby Herakles (He-rak-lees) was born.

Now Queen Hera, the heavenly wife of Zeus, was jealous of all his mortal wives and children. She especially disliked Herakles because it was clear that he was very special to Zeus, and so she thought up all sorts of ways to hurt him. Being jealous can often make people cruel and unkind, and this applied to the gods and goddesses of ancient Greece as well.

Hera nursed so much hatred towards poor Herakles that when he was only a baby, she sent two serpents down to crawl into his crib and strangle him. Hearing an unusual gurgling noise coming from the crib, Alcmena rushed over to find her small son chuckling and squeezing the deadly snakes in his strong little fingers as though they were made of soft wax!

Hera was furious that Herakles had foiled her so easily. And her fury grew no less as the years went by. When Herakles was fully grown, she sent him a far worse torment: a fit of madness which made him kill his own wife and children. Once the fit had passed, and Herakles realised what he had done, he was heartbroken. To try to make up for his crime he agreed to become the servant of a cruel and unpleasant man, King Eurystheus (You-rees-thee-us), and carry out twelve labours for him, all of which were highly dangerous.

The first labour was to kill the Nemean (Ne-mee-an) Lion, a fierce beast which was ravaging the countryside; the second was to kill the Hydra, a many-headed monster; the third was to capture a wild boar; the fourth was to kill the Stymphalian (Stim-fail-ee-an) Birds, whose wings of iron blotted out the sun; the fifth was to chase a wonderful deer with golden antlers and bronze hoofs for a whole year and bring her

back alive; the sixth was to clean out a stable which had housed three thousand oxen for thirty years without ever having been cleaned; the seventh was to capture the mad bull of King Minos of Crete; the eighth was to capture and tame man-eating horses; the ninth was to kill the Queen of the Amazons and win her girdle; the tenth was to kill the three-headed herdsman and his two-headed dog who guarded a giant ox; the eleventh was to kill the dragon who guarded the golden apples of immortality; the twelfth was to go down into the Underworld and capture Cerberus (Serb-er-rus), the three-headed hound of death.

It was Herakles' second labour which explains the crab's position in the stars. The Hydra was a gigantic water snake with nine heads, which lived in a gloomy, swampy marsh. Even its breath was poisonous. Although the monster had terrorised the whole of the region and was thought to be indestructible, Herakles set off with confidence, determined to put an end to this horrible creature.

Luckily for Herakles, the goddess Athene (Ath-ee-nee) wanted to help him and she gave him some good advice.

'Force the Hydra out of its hiding place by pelting it with burning arrows,' she recommended.

He did as she suggested, and as the serpent emerged from its swampy lair, Herakles caught hold of its neck and grasped it tightly. Heaving the writhing beast to the shore, and holding his breath to avoid breathing in the poisonous fumes, he continued to grip the Hydra firmly. The monster twined around his feet, trying to trip him up. Again and again, Herakles battered at its many heads with his club, but no sooner was one crushed, than two more grew in its place.

In the midst of this struggle, Hera looked down from the heavens and laughed. She ordered an enormous crab to scuttle out from the swamp to help the Hydra by digging its claws into Herakles's foot.

Howling with pain, Herakles stamped on the crab furiously, crushing it to death. Then he used his blazing arrows to prevent the Hydra from growing new heads by burning them at their base. With his sharp golden sword, he cut through the monster's necks, and buried the Hydra, still hissing, under a heavy rock.

Once again, Herakles had foiled Hera. All the same, she was grateful for the crab's support. In recognition of its attempt to help her, she set the crab's image among the stars as the constellation of Cancer.

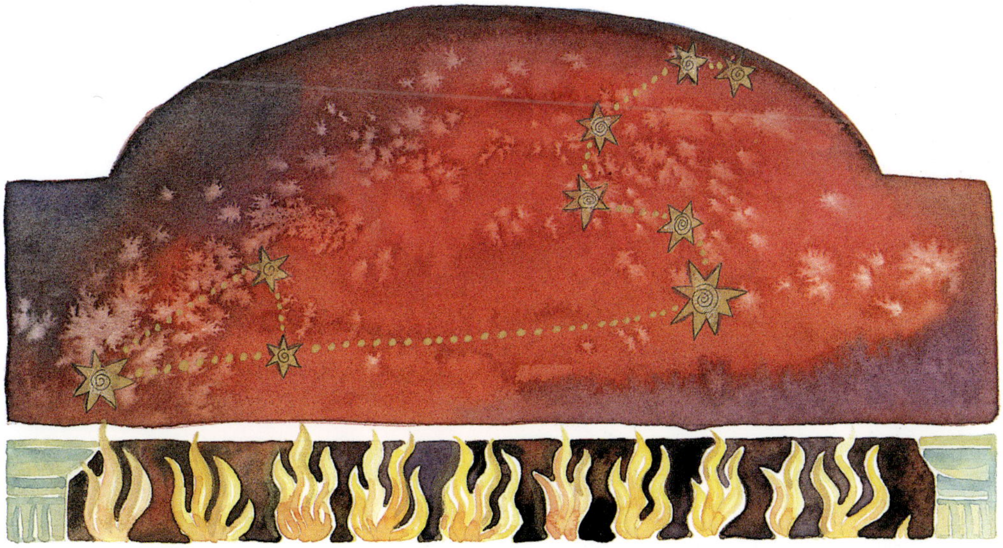

Herakles and the Nemean Lion

LEO (24 JULY–23 AUGUST)

The first labour of Herakles describes his battle with the Nemean Lion, which became the constellation of Leo.

The constellation of Leo also has links with Herakles and his twelve labours because the lion in the stars is the Nemean Lion which Herakles had to fight and kill as his very first labour.

The Nemean Lion was no ordinary beast. Apart from being a lot bigger than an average lion, his pelt was proof against all the known weapons of that time, whether of iron, bronze or stone. Nothing could penetrate the lion's thick skin.

Herakles's first task was to find the lion, which was not easy because the vicious beast had eaten everyone in the surrounding neighbourhood, so there was nobody who could direct Herakles to his den.

However, he eventually tracked the lion down by following the trail of bones of the people and animals the beast had devoured. Catching sight of the lion, Herakles showered a rain of arrows at it, but they just bounced harmlessly back off the animal's thick coat. Herakles only succeeded in angering the beast, which chased him away.

'I'll have to find some other way,' thought Herakles, in desperation.

And then he had a good idea. While the lion was out hunting, Herakles crept into the cave in which the beast lived. There he lay in wait until the lion came home. At last, splattered with blood from his day's killing, the lion returned. Herakles was ready for him. In the dim cave he grabbed his sword and tried to drive it into the lion's heart, but the sword just bent in half.

By now Herakles was growing worried.

'However can I kill this brute?' he muttered.

He tried his club, but it only shattered against the lion's head. Finally, Herakles put his huge hands around the lion's neck and strangled the beast. Then, remembering how wonderfully thick the lion's pelt was, and thinking how protective it would be, he skinned the lion and made himself a cloak with its skin. He used the head as a helmet, so that, when wearing the skin, he could be as invincible as the beast itself once was.

The famous lion was then placed up in the skies by Zeus as the constellation of Leo.

Demeter and Persephone

VIRGO (24 AUGUST–23 SEPTEMBER)

Virgo is associated with the story of Demeter (Dem-ee-ter) and her daughter Persephone (Per-seff-o-nee). For the ancient Greeks, the story of Demeter and Persephone helped to explain why the seasons change.

Demeter was the goddess of the cornfields. She also cherished and protected all young living things. Her long thick hair was the colour of ripe corn and she wore robes that were woven out of the plants and flowers of the meadows. Demeter lived with her lovely daughter Persephone, protected from all the quarrels and problems of the world. Together they took care of nature, making sure that fruit ripened and crops grew. Their life was happy and peaceful; the sun always shone and the flowers always blossomed.

In fact, their life was perfect – until the day when Persephone went to pick flowers all alone. She wandered into a lonely valley where Hades, god of the dead and king of the Underworld, rose up from the Earth in his chariot drawn by two black horses, and caught sight of her.

Hades had long loved Persephone from a distance and had once asked Zeus if he could marry her. Zeus knew that Demeter would not like it if he said 'yes', and that Hades would be angry if he answered with a downright 'no'; so he compromised by neither giving his permission nor refusing it. This gave Hades the opportunity to wait for his chance to spirit Persephone away in secret.

When he found her on her own, he couldn't believe his luck. She looked so charming in her simple white dress clutching armfuls of fragrant flowers, that he couldn't resist her. Without wasting a moment, he scooped her up into his chariot and swept her down into the Underworld to live with him.

Although the Underworld was filled with riches – precious jewels, gold and silver – it was a dank, dark and cheerless place. No sunshine penetrated the kingdom. Persephone missed her mother and was so distressed that she refused to eat or drink.

'I want to go home,' she wept.

Hades was worried. Although he was king of the dead, and ruled a solemn kingdom, he did love Persephone, and her radiant beauty brightened up his dark world. He very much wanted her to stay with him.

'Please, Persephone – do try and eat a little something,' he begged.

Because he seemed so kind and so concerned, Persephone began to relax a little. At last he found something which tempted her – some seeds of a juicy pomegranate fruit. They looked so delicious that Persephone ate six. She did not know that if anyone ate anything in the Underworld, it meant they belonged to Hades for ever.

Meanwhile, on Earth, Demeter was beside herself with worry. She failed in her duties as goddess of the corn. In fact, she refused to let anything on Earth grow until Persephone was found and returned to her. So the Earth grew cold, the crops failed, fruit shrivelled on the trees and the blossoms withered and died. Demeter tore up her clothes, cut off her hair and wandered across the dead land, weeping for her daughter.

By now, the other gods on Olympus were getting worried because the mortals down below were beginning to starve. So Zeus asked Hermes, the winged messenger god, who was both clever and all-seeing, for his help.

First, Hermes paid a flying visit to Earth.

'Lady Demeter,' he said, 'won't you please return to your duties? Earth cannot manage without you – everything is dying.'

'I'm sorry,' Demeter retorted, sternly. 'I care about nothing except finding Persephone safe and sound.'

Next, Hermes went to visit Hades.

'Lord Hades,' he asked, 'will you not let Persephone go back to live with her mother? Life on Earth is getting intolerable without her.'

'No,' said Hades stubbornly. 'I love Persephone and I won't give her up. She makes my sad kingdom joyful.'

'Well,' replied Hermes, 'that does depend on whether she has eaten anything while she has been in your kingdom. If she has not, I have the power to take her back to her mother.'

Hades was triumphant: 'As a matter of fact, she has eaten six pomegranate seeds so she is mine.'

But Hermes was not only a quick-thinking god, he was also very persuasive.

'Now listen, Lord Hades,' he suggested, 'You and Lady Demeter both love Persephone, so why not share her? She has eaten six seeds, so she must stay with you in the Underworld for six months of the year; but for the other six months she may stay with her mother above the earth.'

Hades agreed, while Demeter was so desperate to have her daughter back - even if it was for only half a year - that she too accepted.

So, every autumn, when the crops have been gathered, Persephone leaves for the kingdom of the Underworld. Demeter weeps and the leaves on the trees turn brown and fall with her tears. The Earth turns lifeless and cold for the barren winter months. But, every spring, to celebrate her daughter's homecoming,

Demeter awakens with the sweet-smelling flowers of spring. The animals stir after their long winter sleep and the world comes to life again. Throughout the summer, when Demeter has

her daughter with her, the sun shines, the crops ripen and the flowers bloom. And every year, Persephone's image shines in the early autumn sky as the constellation of Virgo.

The Golden Scales of Dike

LIBRA (24 SEPTEMBER–23 OCTOBER)

The stars that form the golden scales of Libra lie halfway round the band of the zodiac, between Virgo and Scorpio.
Day and night are equal when the Sun passes through the constellation of Libra. The scales are a symbol of balance and equality.

In the time before time began, life was very different from what it is today. The only creatures on Earth were the gods and goddesses and the animals, who lived freely without the interference of humans. But out of the claws of the Scorpion the constellation of Libra, the scales, was born. Dike (Dee-kay), the goddess to whom the scales of justice belonged, was responsible for keeping them in balance.

Then men and women came to live on Earth, alongside the animals. At first, life was good and no one ever argued. But this state of affairs did not last. Soon, people became greedy and selfish. They began quarrelling among themselves; and they began fighting each other in battles for glory and power.

Unable to bear the ugliness of the wars and unhappiness that people caused each other, Dike urged them to live in peace. But her words fell on deaf

ears. The men and women of Earth did not listen. They just carried on squabbling and fighting. For a long time, Dike tried and tried to make them behave fairly and kindly to each other, but it was no use. In the end, even she gave up, retiring to live among the harmonious stars.

Her scales still shine in the heavens as the constellation of Libra, reminding us that we can use them to weigh up the good and the bad in the world, and to judge ourselves and others fairly and wisely.

Orion and the Scorpion

Scorpio (24 October–22 November)

The constellation of the giant scorpion up in the sky is surrounded by a number of stories which involve the mighty hunter Orion – a hero who is represented by another familiar group of stars.

Orion was said to be the tallest and the most handsome man in the world. He was so tall that he could walk the deepest oceans and still his head would be above water. He was often to be seen out hunting in the woods and hills of Greece with his pack of dogs. His constellation shows him striding across the heavens flourishing a gleaming sword on his bejewelled belt.

Many of the stories surrounding the constellations of Orion and Scorpio echo the annual rising and setting of their constellations, which appear to pursue each other across the sky. One story tells how Earth sent the scorpion to sting Orion, to punish him for being boastful.

'I am such a strong and powerful hunter, I could easily rid the Earth of any beast or creature,' Orion had once declared proudly.

'Indeed,' said Earth. 'Try this!'

And up from her breast rose a giant scorpion, full of venom, which stung Orion and immediately sent him to his death.

The scorpion was put up as a constellation by Earth to mark her victory, while Artemis, who had loved Orion, placed his image up in the skies in his own constellation. Because Orion had cared so dearly for his hunting dog, Artemis also put a star up for his dog: this is Sirius (Si-ree-us), the brightest star in the heavens.

There is another story surrounding Orion and the scorpion.

One day, when Orion was out in the woods, he caught sight of seven beautiful sisters, the daughters of Atlas and Pleione (Play-o-nee). Orion loved them all at first sight and began to chase after them. Although Orion was handsome, he was, as you may remember,

very very tall, and the sisters were terrified. They cried out to Zeus to save them.

'Help!' they shrieked. 'Help us, O heavenly Father Zeus – save us!' they screamed in fear.

Zeus heard their pleas and answered their cries for help by turning them, first, into a flock of doves so they could fly away, and later, into the seven stars which are now called the Pleiades.

Some say Orion was stung by the scorpion in punishment for chasing the seven sisters. Zeus decided that the constellations of Orion and the Pleiades should be arranged in the heavens so that Orion would always chase the seven sisters but would never catch up with them – just as Scorpio appears to be in constant pursuit of Orion.

Chiron the Centaur

SAGITTARIUS (23 NOVEMBER–21 DECEMBER)

The constellation of Sagittarius depicts a strange creature called a centaur, which has the body and head of a man, and the hindquarters of a horse. The centaur we call Sagittarius is depicted pointing a bow and arrow high into the sky. He is named after Chiron, king of the centaurs.

In ancient Greece there were many strange creatures: as well as centaurs, there were nymphs, dryads, fauns and satyrs. They were a wild bunch, well known for their noisy parties, and for singing, dancing and merry-making at all hours of the day and night.

The only quiet centaur was Chiron. Chiron's mother was a cloud maiden, so he was semi-divine. He was taught by Apollo, god of the sun (like Helios), and Artemis, goddess of the moon, and from them learned both wisdom and spirituality. He dwelt in a cave high up the rocky, snowy sides of Mount Pelion. He was the oldest and wisest of all the centaurs, with great strength in his horse part, while his white-bearded head was rich with knowledge and experience. In fact, he was so famous that the sons of many kings and heroes, such as Jason, came to him for their education. Chiron gave them lessons in duty; he taught them to fear the gods, to respect old age and to stand by one another in pain and hardship.

Herakles was a good friend of Chiron. Not long after his escapade with the Hydra, he stopped by the centaur's cave to tell him of his latest adventure.

'The Hydra was the most amazing creature, Chiron,' said Herakles. 'Its heads kept reappearing as soon as I crushed them. But I managed to slay it in the end. They say its blood is deadly poisonous, so I thought it would be a good idea to dip my arrows in it. They are bound to come in useful for my future labours, aren't they?'

The friends chatted happily for a while, and finally Herakles took his leave. Unfortunately, as he left the cave, one of the poisoned arrows in his quiver accidentally grazed Chiron's thigh. Howling in pain, Chiron crawled to the back of the cave to see what herbs he could find to heal the wound. If he had been mortal, of course, Chiron would have died immediately, because the Hydra's blood in which the arrow had been dipped was so poisonous. But half of him was divine, so he could not die. He was doomed to live for ever in agony.

Chiron became a very great healer because he learned so much from experimenting with herbs and medicines as he tried to find an antidote to the poison. He also learned great compassion for the pain of others, having experienced so much constant pain himself. He managed to cure many people, but never himself. Eventually Zeus felt so sorry for him that he allowed Chiron to change places with Prometheus (Prom-ee-thee-us), who was the creator of the human race.

Prometheus had made the first men and women out of the red soil of Earth which he moistened with his tears, and he loved his creation dearly. Then Prometheus stole fire from the gods. This meant that the human race would be more like the gods and less like animals. Zeus was very angry indeed with Prometheus because he did not like to think of mortals as being in any way like the gods. So he sentenced Prometheus to a terrible punishment, from which he could be released only if another immortal was prepared to give up everlasting life and offer it to Prometheus. Chiron was so tired of living in constant pain that he was grateful for the opportunity to die and so end his anguish. He gladly gave his immortality to Prometheus and died in his place.

Then Zeus set Chiron's image in the stars as the constellation of Sagittarius.

The Birth of Zeus

CAPRICORN (22 DECEMBER–20 JANUARY)

The constellation of Capricorn is as strange as that of Sagittarius. It is a sea goat, with the head and half the body of a goat, and the tail of a fish. The story of Capricorn is also the story of the birth of Zeus, the father of the gods.

In the very beginning of time, human beings lived in a golden age. The weather was always fine; there were no floods or gales or storms; no one had any cares or worries, and no one had to work hard. The men and women who dwelt on Earth lived in great happiness. They never cooked or cleaned, but just ate the delicious wild strawberries that carpeted the ground and the other fruits of the forest which grew plentifully. No one ever suffered illness or pain and no one ever grew old. People just danced and laughed all day long.

The god Cronus ruled during this happy time and he wanted his reign to last for ever.

'If only,' he wished, 'my golden age might never end.'

To put his mind at rest, he asked an oracle what the future held in store for him.

The oracle spoke thus: 'Father Cronus, your rule will have an end. One day, your son will dethrone you and rule in your place.'

Cronus trembled with fear. 'Whatever can I do to prevent this?' he wondered despairingly. At last, he had an idea. 'I cannot stop my children being born,' he thought. 'But I can stop them growing up!'

So every time his wife, Rhea (Ray-a), gave birth to a child, Cronus promptly swallowed it whole! Rhea had five babies, each of whom her husband gobbled up the moment he set eyes on them.

Rhea was desperately unhappy about losing all her children in this terrible fashion. 'Next time,' she promised herself, 'I will not let it happen.'

So when the time came for her sixth child to be born, she crept softly away at the dead of night. Rhea gave birth to baby Zeus

secretly in a cave on Mount Lycaeum (Ly-kay-um) in Arcadia. She bathed him lovingly in the River Neda, and then called out softly into the dark of the night, 'Please, Mother Earth, look after my baby.'

She left baby Zeus lying in a comfortable little nest of bracken and hurried back to her husband before he could wonder where she was.

'Cronus never looks at our children when they have just been born,' she said to herself. 'He will never notice the difference.' And she wrapped a large stone in baby clothes. 'Here you are, husband,' she said, handing him the bundle. 'Here is your son.'

With a loud snort, Cronus opened his huge mouth and swallowed the stone, baby clothes and all. Rhea smiled a secret smile to herself. She hoped and prayed that her precious baby Zeus would be well looked after.

Her wish was granted, for, in the meantime, Mother Earth had taken the baby to the beautiful island of Crete. There he was nursed and cared for by the kind Amaltheia (A-mal-thay-a), whose name means 'tender'. She was a goat-nymph – that is, half goat and half nymph – and she looked after the young Zeus with the greatest love and devotion, feeding him on her own rich milk and sweet lavender-scented honey. Zeus's golden cradle was hung high upon a tree so that Cronus would not be able to find him in heaven, on Earth or even in the ocean. Young men in armour stood round the cradle, clashing their shields and rattling their swords so that Cronus would not hear the sounds of baby Zeus wailing and become suspicious.

When Zeus was old enough, he set out to find his real mother. When at last they were reunited, Rhea wept tears of joy. 'I am so happy! At last, my son, you have come to free your brothers and sisters,' she cried. 'I have been planning this for years!' So saying, she took Zeus aside and told him of her plan.

'I have told your father that he is to have a new cup-bearer to serve his drinks,' she whispered, 'and you will be that person! Come, I will prepare a potion which I will mix with honey, and you can offer it to your father. He will never suspect a thing.'

Zeus did as his mother told him, offering Cronus the magic drink. Cronus drank deeply and then vomited up first the stone, followed by Zeus's older brothers and sisters, one after the other, all fully grown and quite unhurt. In gratitude, they asked Zeus to be their leader, even though he was younger than they, and together they fought a long bitter war against Cronus.

The war was hard and lasted over ten years, but eventually Cronus was beaten and Zeus became the ruling god in his place. He banished his father to an island in the farthest west, where Cronus ruled as the god of time and old age. His golden age had ended, but it is said that Cronus still waits, and that if he waits patiently enough, the age of gold will one day return.

When Zeus later became lord of the universe, he did not forget his mother-goat, Amaltheia, who had nursed him so lovingly. He took one of her horns and turned it into the horn of plenty, which is always filled with whatever delicious food or drink its owner may wish for, and is never empty. And in recognition for all she had done for him, he set her image among the stars as the constellation of Capricorn.

Ganymede the Cup Bearer

AQUARIUS (21 JANUARY–19 FEBRUARY)

The constellation of Aquarius shows a person pouring water out of a jug. It is thought that the story behind this group of stars is that of Ganymede .

Ganymede (Ga-nee-meed) was the son of King Tros, after whom Troy is named. The young prince was the most exquisite youth who ever lived and was adored and admired by both gods and mortals. Zeus was especially fond of beautiful people, and was very taken with Ganymede's elegant figure, his wonderfully modelled features and gleaming golden hair. Thinking it would be appropriate for so handsome a mortal as Ganymede to live with the gods, Zeus disguised himself as an enormous eagle. He flew down to Earth, captured Ganymede and bore him up to Olympus, to the palace of the gods.

Zeus then had to find him a job, so he decided that Ganymede should be given the special honour of being his personal cup bearer. In order for the gods to remain young and to live for ever, they drank a special type of nectar, and the person who filled their golden cups was known as the cup bearer. The position was highly prized. Until that time, the honour of being cup bearer to the gods had belonged to Hebe (Hee-bee), the daughter of Zeus and Hera.

When his father first discovered that Ganymede was missing, he was distraught. He had no idea what had happened to his dear son or where he could be. He was therefore both surprised and greatly relieved when Hermes, the winged messenger-god, paid him a visit.

'Do not fret, King Tros,' Hermes assured him. 'Your son is safe in the heavens with Father Zeus. He has been given the gift of immortality so he will never have to suffer the miseries of old age, nor will he ever die as ordinary humans do.'

Then Hermes produced some gifts he had been told to offer the king: the first was a vine of pure gold, and the second was a pair of magic white horses which could run over the sea and over the cornfields as swiftly as the wind itself.

'Father Zeus hopes that these fine horses and this golden vine will help to ease the pain of losing your son, King Tros,' said Hermes kindly.

The king accepted the gifts graciously as compensation for the loss of his son's company. Hermes's comforting last words were: 'When I last saw Ganymede, your Majesty, he was smiling, pouring nectar from his golden jug into the cup of the Father of Heaven.'

Indeed, Ganymede lived very contentedly in Olympus, where he was popular with all the gods. He liked being Zeus's favourite servant. But Hera, Queen of Heaven, was not at all pleased.

'How dare you give the honour of being your cup bearer to this Ganymede fellow?' she demanded angrily. 'That privilege always belonged to our daughter, Hebe. You can't just push her out like that!'

Zeus and Hera were always squabbling and trying to outdo one another, and Zeus was keen to score a point over Hera. So he was delighted to add to her annoyance by setting Ganymede's image among the stars as Aquarius, the water carrier.

Aphrodite and the Fish

PISCES (20 FEBRUARY–20 MARCH)

The image of the two fish swimming in different directions make up the constellation of Pisces.
Aphrodite, the goddess of love and beauty, was thought to be responsible for this particular constellation being set in the stars.

After Zeus had fought his father, Cronus, he defeated the race of giants who were the children of Mother Earth. In revenge for the destruction of her children, Mother Earth gave birth to a terrifying monster called Typhon (Ty-fon). He was the largest and most frightening creature ever born. From the thighs down he was a mass of coiled snakes. His arms were so long that when he spread them out they reached a hundred leagues each way, and he had countless snakes' heads instead of hands. His huge head was that of a donkey and he was so tall, he could easily touch the stars. Typhon had mighty black wings which darkened the sun, and fire flashed from his eyes. Whenever he opened his mouth, flaming rocks hurtled out. He was feared by gods and humans alike.

Let loose by Mother Earth, Typhon thundered towards the Olympian home of the gods, declaring war on them all. The gods hurried to disguise themselves, in the hope that Typhon might not notice them. Zeus took the image of a ram; Hera, queen of heaven, a white cow; Artemis, the moon goddess, a cat; and Hermes, the messenger god, an ibis. Ares, god of war, became a boar; Aphrodite, goddess of love, and her son Eros dived deep into the ocean and took the shape of twin fishes.

Only Athene, the goddess of wisdom and war, refused to hide. She taunted Zeus for being a coward until he was so ashamed that he resumed his own form. Zeus then hurled thunderbolts at the monster. A bloody battle followed. Fighting furiously, both Zeus and Typhon were soon wounded and bleeding, but the monster gained an advantage by coiling his snaky body round Zeus for a moment. Typhon took this opportunity to cut out Zeus's sinews. Without these, Zeus could not move and was left lying helpless on the ground.

Typhon, who had also been badly hurt during the struggle, crawled away to a cave to recover, clutching the sinews, which he hid under a pile of goat-skins. Poor Zeus had no choice but to lie there, quite powerless to defend himself should the monster return. Then Hermes and Pan, the goat-god, came looking for him.

Hermes, who was famous for his quick wits, worked on a plan to win those sinews back.

'We need a mortal to help us,' he mused. 'It is no good you, Pan, or me disguising ourselves as humans. After all, Typhon is immortal and he would recognise us immediately.'

Luckily for them, a mortal prince by the name of Cadmus was at that moment wandering through the hills of Thrace. Pan and Hermes hastened to greet him. 'You will be a great king and your children will be famous,' they promised, 'but first you must help Zeus. He is in dire need.'

Hermes gave Cadmus some goat-skins to disguise himself as a simple shepherd, and Pan lent him a flock of sheep and his magical pipes. The music of Pan's pipes is far sweeter and more magical than any human instrument.

'Use music to soothe Typhon,' Hermes and Pan told Cadmus, 'and then you can retrieve the sinews.'

Nervously, Cadmus made his way to the cave where the injured monster lay, trying to recover, so that he could strike again. As he approached, Cadmus played the magic pipes. Typhon listened, and what he heard was so breathtakingly lovely that he made no move to hurt what he took to be a simple mortal shepherd.

'Come closer, lad,' he muttered. 'Play to me so that the sweetness of your music will make me forget my wounds, and heal me.'

'If you like the music of my pipes,' said Cadmus, 'you would simply adore the music of my lyre. Even the sun god Apollo himself cannot play the lyre as well as I do.'

'Then play the lyre,' roared Typhon impatiently.

'I'm afraid I can't,' mumbled Cadmus, pretending to be upset, 'because when Apollo heard me play, he was so jealous that he snatched away my lyre and broke all the strings. Look!' And Cadmus showed him a broken lyre. 'Unless I can find some gut to string it, I fear I can never again play the most beautiful music in the world.'

Typhon crawled to the back of the cave and brought out Zeus's sinews.

'Here, take these – I'm sure they will do – and then play to me,' he grunted.

'Why, thank you, sir – I most certainly will. I will work on the lyre tonight, and tomorrow you will hear its melody. But for now, let me lull you to sleep with my pipes.'

Before the monster had time to think, Cadmus played a soothing lullaby so that the great creature immediately grew drowsy, and very soon began to snore.

Holding tightly to the precious sinews, Cadmus made his way back to Zeus, who swiftly fitted the sinews back into his limbs. In a flash, his strength was restored. He leapt into his chariot, ready to do battle with his enemy once more.

Zeus pelted the sleeping monster with thunderbolts and Typhon, as he tried to escape, tripped and fell into the sea not far from Italy. Zeus picked up the island of Sicily and threw it down on top of him.

And there Typhon lies, imprisoned, even to this day, in the roots of Mount Etna. Sometimes he still writhes and shouts out in anger, sending his fiery breath up through the volcano.

After the battle, the other gods and goddesses resumed their own forms. Aphrodite and her son Eros gave special thanks to the fish whose shapes they had taken to protect them from Typhon. To show her gratitude, Aphrodite set their images in the stars as the constellation of Pisces.

The Sun Signs

Ancient men and women saw the universe, the earth and the people living on it as being connected, and being made up of the four elements of Fire, Earth, Air and Water. Each of the elements governs three signs of the zodiac.

Fire

The element of fire represents the power of the imagination. Daydreams, games, fantasies - all of these are associated with the fiery signs. So if you are born with one or more of the fiery signs in your birth chart, you will find it easy and natural to express your imagination creatively.

ARIES THE RAM

21 March - 20 April

Aries, the first sign of the zodiac, is connected with beginnings. Aries is ruled by Mars, the god of war. Ariens are often argumentative, headstrong and short-tempered. They are also romantic, brave and full of good ideas, with great enthusiasm for change.

Ariens are very competitive but they are also willing to help the less fortunate. If life is too dull and routine, Ariens will get very bored and rebel. As long as things are moving, they are happy. Because Ariens are so optimistic and positive, they usually manage to draw others in to share their dreams. And because they are such fun to be with it is difficult to be annoyed with an Arien for long.

LEO THE LION

24 July - 23 August

The sun passes through Leo at the height of summer and reflects the warmth and generosity of those born at this time. The lion is the king of beasts and Leos, if not royal, see themselves at least as different and superior. The sun rules this sign.

Leos need to find something they can shine at so they can always be seen as special. If they are not admired or looked up to they feel very despondent and may lack a sense of purpose. Leos also make good teachers - they love an audience and they can make anything interesting.

SAGITTARIUS THE ARCHER

23 November - 21 December

The sun travels through Sagittarius when the days of winter grow darker. Outside activities are curtailed and the imagination is more important than ever. Ruled by the expansive god Jupiter, Sagittarius is a sign full of creativity, hope and optimism. Even when things go wrong, Sagittarians find a positive reason for it. Nothing is ever wasted; no experience, no matter how painful, is written off as useless. The Sagittarian spirit is restless and searching, always looking out for an opportunity for growth and new experience. Sagittarians constantly need to be discovering new horizons. Sagittarius is a sign that is traditionally associated with being lucky, but really the good fortune of Sagittarians comes from their willingness to take risks as well as to take advantage of all opportunities as they present themselves.

Earth

The Greeks imagined the earth to be the living body of a great goddess, Gaia. They thought everything that lived and grew was born from her and was returned to her at the end of life. These qualities are reflected in the cycles of nature. The year starts with the birth of new buds in spring. This new life ripens in summer, withers in autumn and remains dormant in winter, coming alive again the following spring. Like the natural world, those who are born under the earthy signs work steadily at their own pace, disliking to be pushed or rushed, for nature has its own time frame.

TAURUS THE BULL

21 April - 21 May

As the sun passes through Taurus in late spring, the earth is growing warm. Young animals are born and spring flowers are blooming. Taurus is ruled by Venus, goddess of love and beauty. Taureans are peaceful and gentle, content to let life unfold gradually. They are placid, patient and kind-hearted, quick to help others, slow to anger. Like the bull, they are happy to graze in a meadow of rich grass, unruffled unless they are provoked. But when they do lose their temper they let go completely.

Taureans enjoy the comforts and luxuries of life. They appreciate fine music, beautiful surroundings, soft fabrics, good perfume and delicious food. Taureans value money because of the beautiful things it can buy them.

VIRGO THE VIRGIN

24 August - 23 September

The sun passes through Virgo in early autumn, at harvest time. Virgo is ruled by Mercury, the messenger god who was known for his sharp wit. Those born under this sign use their minds well. Like the earth herself, Virgos are efficient and thorough in everything they do. They like things to be well-organised and smoothly run. They are sometimes teased for being too nit-picking and fussy, but it is their way of making sure that things are properly done.

Virgos usually need to feel useful and like to help other people. They are reliable, thoughtful and patient, but while they are willing to help others, they can find it quite difficult to ask for help for themselves. Virgos often care about health and hygiene. They tend to choose foods that are nourishing and wholesome.

CAPRICORN THE MOUNTAIN GOAT

22 December - 20 January

The sun moves into Capricorn when the world is at its most wintry. Capricorn is ruled by Saturn, the god of patience, time and old age. Capricorns are determined and disciplined and work hard for what they get. Young Capricorns can worry too much, but this gets better with age. Capricorns are often concerned about how others see them. They are ambitious and competitive, but in a very dignified manner. They concentrate calmly and persevere quietly until they win.

Capricorns take responsibilities very seriously. They do what they say they are going to do and can be relied upon completely. They tend to put work before play, methodically working within the limits all the time. On the outside Capricorns look cool, calm and collected, but they are easily hurt and rejected. They can be hard to get to know, but once they make a firm friendship, they are loyal to the end.

Air

For the Greeks, air was the realm of the gods, who lived in splendour high above the earth. Air is a symbol of understanding. Humans are able to plan, think ahead and make decisions. The element of air reflects the mind's ability to sort out experiences and form ideas.

GEMINI THE TWINS

22 May - 21 June

The sun passes through Gemini in the early summer, when the earth is at her liveliest. The weather is warm and nature is alive and buzzing. Gemini is ruled by Mercury, the god of communication and messages. Those born under this sign love to chat, gossip and exchange ideas. They are usually good at written communication too.

This sign is sometimes called "the butterfly of the zodiac" because Geminians flit from one idea to another. Geminians are inquisitive, curious and keen to keep themselves informed. They generally know a little about a lot, but they very rarely become deeply absorbed into any one subject. Geminians have quick-witted and versatile minds, but as they get easily bored, they need constant mental stimulation and must be stretched all the time.

LIBRA THE SCALES

24 September - 23 October

The sun passes through Libra in late autumn, when day and night are equal. Libra is a peace-loving sign ruled by Venus, goddess of love and beauty. Librans appreciate beauty in art and nature. They are good designers of clothes or houses as they usually have a fine sense of colour and style. Harmony in material surroundings is important to Librans.

Librans find it difficult to make decisions because they can always see both sides of any point of view. It is also very important to them to be well-thought of by others so they tend to agonise over friendships. Librans fight for their ideal of a perfect world, believing that people are capable of being truly good. They are sensitive to criticism and easily hurt.

AQUARIUS THE WATER CARRIER

21 January - 19 February

The sun passes through Aquarius during the bleakest winter months. This sign is ruled by the sky-god Uranus. Aquarians have brilliant visions about what the world could be like, but they are often disappointed when their visions are not realised as perfectly as they had imagined.

Aquarians have a great sense of community. But, although they love the idea of making the world a better place, they are not always very interested in any one person's problems. They would rather design a shopping centre with a moving pavement than carry a basket across the street for an old lady!

Aquarians are very loyal and generous to those people and causes that they value. Often unconventional, they are always prepared to listen to new ideas. They tend to make equally good pupils and teachers because of their genuine love of learning and their wish to pass on that knowledge to others.

Water Signs

Water is the element from which much of life on earth emerges. It can take the shape of whatever container it is carried in, for it has no shape of its own. The water signs are connected with the feelings, so people with their sun in a water sign are often well aware of how they are feeling. The water signs are also sensitive to other people's feelings.

CANCER THE CRAB

22 June - 23 July

The sun passes through Cancer in mid-summer. The crops and fruit are ripening and many flowers are at their most beautiful. Ruled by the moon, which is a symbol of the mother, Cancerians make good parents. Most Cancerians consider their home and their family to be a top priority.

Like the crab, Cancerians often have a tough outer shell that can conceal a very soft inside. Crabs zig-zag from side to side. Cancerians, too, are usually very subtle about how they go about getting things, not approaching what they want directly, but taking a more side-stepping path.

Imagination and sensitivity are typical of the Cancerian personality, as well as moods, which tend to change frequently. The phases of the moon govern the ebb and flow of tides, and Cancerians are sensitive to these changes.

SCORPIO THE SCORPION

24 October - 22 November

Scorpio corresponds to the fading strength of the sun as the earth prepares for the long winter nights. This sign is ruled by Pluto, the god of the underworld.

Scorpions are passionate and feel things very deeply. They are also extremely loyal and are capable of devotion and self-sacrifice to those they love. They feel very strongly about anything they do, from projects to hobbies and interests - whatever they are engaged in is given their fullest attention. Like the crab, the scorpion has a hard outer shell which protects a soft, vulnerable inside. Even though Scorpios may appear tough and cool, their feelings are tender.

PISCES THE FISH

20 February - 20 March

The sun moves through Pisces in the last phase of winter. Ruled by Neptune, god of the ocean, Pisceans are gentle, dreamy, intuitive and sensitive.

Pisceans are very vulnerable. They dislike being limited by rules and boundaries and have a great longing to be part of a greater whole. They are very idealistic, very in love with the idea of love, and long for romance and happy endings. They are highly creative, particularly in drama, theatre and film. Pisceans want above all to be with others without any arguments. They have a strong drive to help and are often sympathetic to other people's pain.

Pisceans thrive on change and variety. They don't mind too much about material comforts. For the Piscean, the real prison would be a world where there is no possibility for change and no scope for the imagination.